Microsoft Copilot AI
Redefining Productivity and Human Interaction

Why This Cutting-Edge Technology Will Make You Rethink Your Digital World

Alejandro S. Diego

Copyright © Alejandro S. Diego, 2024.

All rights reserved. No part of this publication may be reproduced, distributed, or transmitted in any form or by any means, including photocopying, recording, or other electronic or mechanical methods, without the prior written permission of the publisher, except in the case of brief quotations embodied in critical reviews and certain other noncommercial uses permitted by copyright law.

Table of Contents

Introduction...3
Chapter 1: The AI Revolution at Microsoft................6
Chapter 2: Unveiling Think Deeper..........................14
Chapter 3: The Breakthrough of Copilot Vision......22
Chapter 4: Enhancing Human-AI Conversations with Copilot Voice...31
Chapter 5: Copilot Daily: Personalized Briefings at Your Fingertips...42
Chapter 6: The Hardware Behind Copilot: Co-Pilot Plus PCs..52
Chapter 7: Windows 11 24H2 Update: Elevating the AI Experience...63
       You said:.. 68
       ChatGPT said:..68
Chapter 8: Privacy and Security: Microsoft's Commitment..80
Chapter 9: Microsoft's AI Ecosystem: The Power of Integration..92
Chapter 10: The Future of AI with Microsoft Copilot..106
Conclusion..122

Introduction

Microsoft's journey into artificial intelligence has been nothing short of groundbreaking. The tech giant has always been at the forefront of innovation, but its dive into AI has redefined how technology integrates with everyday life. Early on, Microsoft recognized the vast potential AI held—not just for automation but for enhancing human capabilities. With investments in AI research, partnerships, and acquisitions, the company gradually began incorporating AI into its extensive suite of products, from Microsoft Office to Azure, creating smarter solutions for businesses and individuals alike.

However, it wasn't until the introduction of Copilot that Microsoft truly showcased its ability to humanize AI. Initially, Copilot began as a productivity tool, designed to assist users with tasks, automate processes, and streamline workflows. It was an impressive leap forward, offering new ways to tackle mundane work. Yet, as AI capabilities expanded, so did the vision for

Copilot. Microsoft transformed it into much more than a simple assistant. It evolved into a digital companion—one that could understand, anticipate, and even adapt to the unique needs of users.

This shift was not just about enhancing productivity but about redefining the interaction between humans and machines. Copilot began to learn from users, moving beyond simple commands and responses to engage with more intuitive, context-aware interactions. It became clear that Copilot wasn't just another AI-driven tool but a partner in getting things done, designed to think deeper and assist in ways that traditional AI tools couldn't.

The purpose of this book is to delve deep into this transformation—exploring how Microsoft's Copilot is not only reshaping productivity but also changing the very nature of human-AI interaction. From handling complex problem-solving tasks to understanding the context of what's happening on your screen in real-time, Copilot has revolutionized the way we work, communicate, and interact with technology. As AI continues to become an integral part of daily life, understanding the innovations behind Copilot helps us see the broader picture of where AI is heading and how it will shape the future of technology and human interaction.

Chapter 1: The AI Revolution at Microsoft

Microsoft's AI ecosystem is a vast and interconnected network of technologies designed to enhance every aspect of work and life. As a pioneer in the field, Microsoft has consistently pushed the boundaries of artificial intelligence, leveraging its extensive resources and research capabilities to create solutions that are deeply integrated into its platforms. Whether through personal productivity tools or enterprise-level systems, Microsoft's AI touches millions of users worldwide, streamlining tasks, improving decision-making, and automating routine processes.

The foundation of Microsoft's AI ecosystem lies in its ability to embed intelligent features across its entire suite of products. Through platforms like Microsoft Office, Azure, and Windows, AI has been seamlessly woven into the fabric of everyday tools. In Microsoft Word and Excel, for example, AI-powered features like text predictions, data insights, and automated formatting enable users to work faster and more efficiently. These tools no longer serve merely as static applications but as dynamic, intelligent systems that can predict user needs, offer real-time suggestions, and learn from interactions.

One of the most notable advancements in Microsoft's AI ecosystem is its integration into the workplace. Microsoft Teams, a hub for teamwork and communication, has leveraged AI to make virtual collaboration smoother and more effective. With features such as automatic transcription, real-time translation, and intelligent meeting scheduling, AI ensures that users can focus on the content of their discussions rather than the mechanics of arranging them. The application of AI in this space has bridged communication gaps, making it easier for teams across the globe to collaborate in real time, regardless of language or time zones.

Beyond personal productivity, Microsoft has also incorporated AI into broader societal functions.

Through Azure AI, the company's cloud-based platform, industries such as healthcare, finance, and manufacturing have benefited from AI-driven insights and automation. In healthcare, AI helps medical professionals by analyzing vast datasets, enabling earlier disease detection and personalized treatments. In finance, AI-powered fraud detection algorithms analyze transactions at lightning speed, safeguarding users from potential threats. These integrations demonstrate Microsoft's commitment to using AI not just for business efficiency but for broader societal impact.

At the core of this ecosystem is Microsoft's focus on making AI accessible and usable for everyone. AI is no longer seen as a technology reserved for specialized experts but as a tool that enhances the everyday experiences of people in various sectors. Whether through voice recognition in Cortana or image recognition in the Photos app, Microsoft has embedded AI into tools that are used by millions of people without them even realizing it.

The company's vision is clear: AI should enhance daily life without complicating it. By making AI intuitive, user-friendly, and deeply integrated into familiar products, Microsoft has ensured that its AI ecosystem remains accessible, powerful, and transformative for individuals and businesses alike. The seamless integration of AI into daily tasks signals a future where technology becomes a natural extension of human capability, making work and life more efficient, more intelligent, and more connected.

Copilot has emerged as one of the most powerful examples of how AI can fundamentally change productivity. Initially conceived as a tool to assist users in tasks like scheduling, drafting emails, and organizing workflows, it has since evolved into something much more profound. Copilot acts as a dynamic extension of the user's abilities, seamlessly integrating with familiar platforms like Microsoft Office, Outlook, and Teams, transforming how individuals and businesses approach daily work. It is no longer just a passive tool that responds to commands—it anticipates needs, adapts to user behavior, and makes intelligent suggestions that can significantly reduce time spent on routine tasks.

At its core, Copilot's primary function is to simplify complex processes. It can parse vast amounts of information, summarizing documents, generating insights, and even automating repetitive tasks such as scheduling meetings or pulling relevant data from spreadsheets. This AI-driven enhancement means that users can focus on strategic and creative work rather than getting bogged down in manual, time-consuming activities. What sets Copilot apart from traditional productivity tools is its ability to learn from user interactions, becoming more personalized and intuitive over time. Its capacity for real-time adaptation means that it doesn't just perform tasks—it becomes a trusted digital partner that actively contributes to work efficiency.

Central to Copilot's evolution is Microsoft's decision to create **Copilot Labs,** a dedicated space for the most advanced AI experiments and testing. Copilot Labs is where Microsoft pushes the boundaries of what its AI can do, exploring new ways to integrate artificial intelligence into real-world applications. This initiative allows Microsoft to test cutting-edge features with a select group of users—primarily professionals and power users—before rolling them out to a broader audience. The experimental tools in Copilot Labs are designed to handle more complex, nuanced tasks that go beyond simple productivity enhancements.

One such feature is **Think Deeper**, a tool within Copilot Labs that allows the AI to process and respond to more complicated queries by taking the time to generate detailed, step-by-step solutions. This is a marked shift from the rapid, surface-level responses typically associated with AI assistants. For example, instead of merely providing a quick answer to a basic question, Think Deeper can analyze more complex problems, such as planning a multi-phase project or comparing different financial scenarios, and offer a well-thought-out, comprehensive solution. This ability to slow down and consider the intricacies of a challenge is what makes Copilot so revolutionary in the realm of AI-driven productivity.

The birth of Copilot Labs represents Microsoft's commitment to refining and perfecting its AI tools before releasing them to the general public. By allowing users to test experimental features, Microsoft gains valuable feedback on how these advanced tools perform in real-world environments. This user-centered approach ensures that new capabilities are rigorously tested and optimized, resulting in a more polished and reliable experience once they are available on a larger scale. Copilot Labs functions as a breeding ground for innovation, where ideas are explored, tested, and refined before they make their way into the broader Microsoft ecosystem.

The combination of Copilot's role in driving productivity and the forward-thinking experimentation in Copilot Labs signifies a new era in how AI interacts with and supports human work. It is not just about making processes faster or more efficient; it's about fundamentally changing the way we think about work itself, pushing AI to take on more complex roles and responsibilities in both personal and professional environments.

Chapter 2: Unveiling Think Deeper

Think Deeper is one of the most innovative features to come out of Microsoft's Copilot Labs, designed specifically to tackle the complexities of problem-solving in ways that standard AI systems cannot. In many AI-driven tools, responses are often quick, concise, and efficient, but they lack depth when it comes to addressing more complicated scenarios. Think Deeper was created to address this limitation, offering users a way to engage with AI on a deeper level, especially when faced with challenges that require more than just surface-level solutions.

The need for complex problem-solving in AI has been increasingly apparent as users expect more from their digital assistants. Traditional AI tools can handle basic tasks such as setting reminders, summarizing documents, or performing simple calculations. However, when it comes to more intricate problems—like planning a multi-stage project, analyzing data sets with numerous variables, or considering long-term logistical challenges—these basic AI responses fall short. Users need AI that can think critically, weigh various factors, and provide comprehensive answers rather than quick fixes.

This is where Think Deeper steps in. Rather than offering rapid responses designed to get a task done quickly, Think Deeper allows Copilot to slow down and take the necessary time to analyze the complexities of a given problem. For instance, imagine you're planning a home renovation that involves balancing costs, timelines, contractor availability, and material selection. Instead of offering a simplistic answer or pulling up a basic set of options, Think Deeper processes all these elements, comparing different scenarios in detail. It considers the variables, runs through potential outcomes, and delivers a thoughtful, structured plan that accounts for every nuance of the project.

What sets Think Deeper apart from traditional AI tools is its ability to engage in more detailed reasoning and provide step-by-step answers. In contrast to typical AI systems that give quick but often shallow results, Think Deeper can address layers of complexity in a single query. It's particularly useful for professionals dealing with high-stakes decisions or long-term projects where each detail matters. By offering in-depth analysis, Think Deeper empowers users to make better-informed decisions, knowing that the AI has considered all possible angles before providing an answer.

Think Deeper is also an excellent example of how AI can be trained to think in a more human-like way. While most AI tools focus on immediate efficiency, Think Deeper recognizes that some problems benefit from patience and deeper contemplation. This shift towards more thoughtful AI responses marks a turning point in the development of AI technology, moving away from just fast, transactional interactions and towards a model where AI is seen as a collaborative partner in solving complex challenges.

In professional environments, this feature is invaluable. For example, a project manager juggling multiple clients and conflicting deadlines can use Think Deeper to simulate different scheduling options, comparing the risks and benefits of each timeline. Similarly, in financial decision-making, where each choice has far-reaching consequences, Think Deeper can analyze various financial models, compare investment outcomes, and recommend the most prudent course of action.

By moving beyond surface-level responses, Think Deeper expands the capabilities of AI, allowing users to engage with it as they would with a knowledgeable advisor. It transforms AI from a simple assistant into a sophisticated partner, one that can navigate complexity and help users solve problems that require more than just quick answers. This shift signals a future where AI doesn't just save time, but also adds value by providing richer, more meaningful insights tailored to the user's needs.

Think Deeper's capability shines most when applied to real-world situations where complexity is key, and quick, surface-level answers won't suffice. One of the standout applications of this feature is in home renovation projects. Renovations often involve a dizzying array of variables—balancing budgets, sourcing materials, coordinating with contractors, and adjusting timelines. Instead of offering a simple list of contractors or a basic budget plan, Think Deeper can analyze the entire project holistically. It can help determine how changing one aspect, like material selection, might impact the overall cost, project duration, or quality. By comparing various options in detail, Think Deeper provides a step-by-step guide that helps users navigate the complexities of such projects without missing any critical elements.

Another powerful application of Think Deeper is in cost analysis. Businesses and individuals alike are often faced with choices that involve weighing multiple financial factors. For instance, a company looking to expand might need to compare the costs of opening new locations in different regions. Rather than just giving a surface-level overview of the costs, Think Deeper digs into the details, considering variables like real estate prices, local labor costs, tax incentives, and long-term growth potential. This kind of detailed comparison allows users to make informed decisions with a clearer understanding of the financial implications over time.

The power of Think Deeper isn't confined to just these areas—its potential spans industries and use cases. In healthcare, it could assist medical professionals in developing treatment plans by comparing various approaches and their outcomes based on patient history and medical data. In the education sector, it might help administrators analyze the long-term benefits and challenges of different curriculum models. The ability to handle these kinds of nuanced problems, across a wide range of fields, makes Think Deeper a transformative tool in the realm of AI-driven productivity.

The rollout of Think Deeper has been carefully controlled to ensure it meets the needs of real-world users. Microsoft began by introducing the feature to a select group of professional users in five countries: the United States, the United Kingdom, Canada, Australia, and New Zealand. This phased release allows Microsoft to gather feedback from power users in these regions before expanding it globally. The initial feedback has been crucial for refining the feature, ensuring it works seamlessly in different industries and across diverse use cases.

In each of these countries, Think Deeper has been tested by users who rely on AI to make more complex, high-stakes decisions in their everyday work. Microsoft has focused on ensuring that the AI not only provides accurate, in-depth answers but also does so efficiently, allowing users to trust the system as a reliable partner in decision-making. These early tests in real-world scenarios have provided valuable insights, helping Microsoft fine-tune Think Deeper before it is rolled out more broadly.

By carefully monitoring its performance in these countries, Microsoft is ensuring that Think Deeper can handle the full range of challenges that users face in various industries. This global testing phase is a critical step toward refining the AI's ability to navigate complex problems across cultures and business environments, making sure that when Think Deeper reaches a wider audience, it is a polished, effective tool that can adapt to the needs of users worldwide.

Chapter 3: The Breakthrough of Copilot Vision

Copilot Vision is one of Microsoft's most forward-thinking advancements in the realm of AI, marking a significant departure from traditional text-based inputs. While many AI tools respond solely to written commands or queries, Copilot Vision expands the AI's capabilities by allowing it to interpret and interact with what users are seeing on their screens in real time. This revolutionary feature enables the AI to understand not just the words that users type, but the broader context of their activities, transforming how people engage with digital content.

Imagine working on a project in Microsoft Edge or browsing an article online, and instead of typing out a specific question, Copilot Vision is able to analyze the page you are viewing and proactively offer relevant assistance. Whether you're reading a complex research paper, reviewing a financial report, or drafting a document, Copilot Vision recognizes the content on the screen and provides suggestions or insights based on what you're actively engaging with. This allows users to receive more intuitive, contextually aware support, without the need to constantly input text queries.

This real-time screen interaction sets Copilot Vision apart from other AI tools. By "seeing" what the user is working on, it becomes more integrated into the workflow, understanding not just isolated pieces of information but how they fit into the bigger picture. For example, if you're drafting an email while also reviewing a set of meeting notes, Copilot Vision can pull key data from the notes and suggest relevant points to include in your email. Similarly, if you're analyzing a webpage, the AI can provide insights or even suggest follow-up actions, such as finding more resources or drafting a summary of the page.

One of the most powerful elements of Copilot Vision is its ability to interpret a wide variety of content, including websites, documents, and even images. Let's say you're working on a presentation and need to reference multiple reports; Copilot Vision can scan the documents on your screen, extract the most important data, and offer suggestions for how to incorporate it into your slides. This level of real-time interaction turns Copilot from a passive assistant into an active collaborator, helping you manage tasks across multiple platforms seamlessly.

Moreover, Copilot Vision's capacity to understand the broader context of your work goes beyond merely responding to direct commands. It can recognize patterns in how you work, learn your preferences, and adapt its responses to suit your needs more accurately. This makes the interaction between users and the AI feel more natural, as the AI is no longer confined to waiting for input but can instead anticipate user needs based on what's happening in real time.

Despite its advanced capabilities, Copilot Vision has been designed with user privacy in mind. It operates on an opt-in basis, ensuring that it only functions when users actively choose to engage it. None of the data from interactions is stored or used for further training purposes, and once the session is closed, all data from that session is permanently discarded. This allows users to leverage the full potential of the tool while maintaining control over their privacy and data security.

Copilot Vision represents a major leap forward in how AI can assist users, not just by responding to commands but by actively participating in the user's work process. By seeing beyond text inputs and understanding the context of what is on the screen, Copilot Vision makes interactions smoother, more efficient, and more intuitive. This is a significant step in the evolution of AI, offering users a richer, more integrated experience that reshapes how we approach tasks and manage information in real time.

As with any advanced technology that interacts closely with user data, privacy concerns are at the forefront of discussions surrounding Copilot Vision.

Microsoft has taken a proactive approach to addressing these concerns, ensuring that users retain full control over how and when Copilot Vision operates. Given that Copilot Vision can analyze and interact with the content on a user's screen, Microsoft has implemented strict privacy safeguards to ensure that this powerful tool doesn't overstep boundaries or compromise sensitive information.

One of the key aspects of Copilot Vision's privacy protection is its **opt-in** nature. Unlike some AI tools that operate automatically in the background, Copilot Vision only becomes active when the user chooses to enable it. This gives users the autonomy to decide when and how the AI will assist them. At no point does Copilot Vision monitor activities without explicit permission, ensuring that it respects the user's preferences from the start.

Once activated, Copilot Vision operates in a highly secure manner. Microsoft has implemented a system where **no data is stored or shared** once the session ends. As soon as the user completes their interaction with Copilot Vision, all the data from that session is permanently discarded, and nothing is retained for future use or training purposes. This policy ensures that there is no possibility of sensitive information being misused or accessed later, further reinforcing user trust.

Additionally, Microsoft has limited the scope of Copilot Vision's interactions by pre-approving a set list of websites and applications with which the AI can engage. For example, if you're browsing a website that has a paywall or contains sensitive information, Copilot Vision is programmed not to interact with or analyze such content. This ensures that the AI doesn't overreach into areas where privacy might be a concern or where content restrictions apply. This thoughtful limitation provides an additional layer of security, giving users confidence that the AI will not interact with or expose sensitive materials unintentionally.

Beyond the technical measures, Microsoft has integrated clear communication into Copilot Vision's design. Users are always aware when the AI is active, what it is interacting with, and when it ceases to function. By providing transparency about how the tool operates, Microsoft addresses many of the common fears surrounding AI's role in privacy. These features reflect Microsoft's broader commitment to privacy, ensuring that users feel secure when using Copilot Vision as a trusted assistant in their work.

In terms of use case scenarios, Copilot Vision offers personalized assistance in a wide range of practical settings by analyzing what's happening on your screen in real-time. One common scenario is when users are working on multiple tasks at once, such as drafting documents, sending emails, or reviewing reports. Copilot Vision can instantly recognize what's on your screen and suggest actions or content relevant to your task. For instance, if you are drafting a report while simultaneously reviewing data from a spreadsheet, Copilot Vision can extract the most important figures from the data and suggest ways to incorporate them into your report, without you needing to switch between applications.

In another scenario, imagine you're reading an article on Microsoft Edge about a specific topic and want to dig deeper into a particular section. Copilot Vision can analyze the article and offer additional information, such as related articles or references, saving you the time and effort of manually searching for supplementary resources. This ability to assist in context makes the workflow smoother and allows users to focus on the bigger picture rather than getting bogged down in minor details.

A more advanced use case involves Copilot Vision interacting with images and documents. If you're working on a design project, for example, Copilot Vision can analyze a series of visual elements and offer insights on layout, design consistency, or suggest improvements based on recognized patterns in successful projects. Similarly, if you're dealing with large contracts or legal documents, the AI can scan for key terms, flag important sections, or summarize long paragraphs, reducing the time spent manually combing through the text.

By being aware of what's happening on your screen, Copilot Vision offers truly personalized assistance, making it feel less like a generic tool and more like a tailored assistant that fits your workflow. This kind of smart interaction helps users handle tasks more efficiently, while also learning to anticipate user needs based on the context of what's being worked on, all within a framework that prioritizes privacy and security. The balance of personalization and protection is what sets Copilot Vision apart from other AI tools, making it a powerful and secure ally in navigating digital tasks.

Chapter 4: Enhancing Human-AI Conversations with Copilot Voice

One of the most common criticisms of traditional AI interactions is their robotic nature. While AI systems have become remarkably advanced in processing information and delivering responses, they often lack the fluidity and natural feel of human conversations. The disjointed, mechanical tone of these interactions can make even the most sophisticated AI tools feel impersonal and inefficient, especially when users expect real-time, natural communication.

Traditional AI systems typically rely on predefined commands or structured inputs, which can result in rigid conversations. Users often find themselves needing to phrase questions in specific ways to elicit useful responses. Additionally, these systems can struggle with interruptions, changes in context, or deviations from a standard query. As a result, interactions can feel more like working with an automated script rather than engaging in a meaningful dialogue.

Copilot Voice was designed specifically to address this gap, bringing a new level of conversational fluidity and human-like interaction to the AI experience. Unlike older systems, Copilot Voice doesn't just respond to input; it can interpret natural language, adapt to changes in conversation, and allow for more seamless, real-time exchanges. The result is an AI that feels less like a machine and more like a responsive digital companion.

One of the key ways Copilot Voice achieves this is through its ability to process and respond to conversations in a more dynamic and flexible manner. For example, if a user is in the middle of giving instructions or asking a question but changes their mind halfway through, Copilot Voice can adjust to the shift without becoming confused or requiring the user to restart. This makes the interaction feel more natural, as humans often change direction in conversation based on new thoughts or insights. The AI's ability to keep up with these shifts eliminates the frustration that often comes with having to repeat or rephrase requests when dealing with traditional AI.

Additionally, Copilot Voice significantly reduces the delay that is typical of AI systems, where users might ask a question and then have to wait for a response. The quicker, more fluid responses from Copilot Voice help to maintain the momentum of conversations, making the experience feel more like talking to a real person. This responsiveness is particularly beneficial in fast-paced work environments where users need quick answers without long pauses, such as when making on-the-fly decisions or collaborating on projects.

Copilot Voice also allows for **interruptions** and **redirections** during a conversation without losing track of the context. Imagine being in a situation where you're asking the AI to summarize a document, but halfway through, you remember a related question or want to shift focus to a different document. With older AI systems, this kind of interruption could derail the process, forcing you to start over. However, Copilot Voice can handle these mid-conversation changes effortlessly, recognizing that conversations, like real-life discussions, are often non-linear.

Beyond handling these interruptions, Copilot Voice also improves the tone and quality of the interaction. Instead of sounding robotic or overly formal, Copilot Voice is designed to mimic the natural rhythm, pacing, and tone of human conversations. It uses more natural phrasing and can even incorporate small conversational cues, such as acknowledging your input with a simple "Got it" or asking follow-up questions that feel intuitive rather than scripted. This conversational style is crucial in reducing the barrier between users and AI, making it feel more like a dialogue than a command-response interaction.

The value of this smooth, human-like interaction extends beyond just making conversations feel more natural. For users who rely on multitasking, Copilot Voice becomes an even more indispensable tool. Whether it's during a busy workday where hands-free interaction is critical or while managing multiple projects, the ability to speak naturally to the AI without structuring inputs or waiting for delayed responses saves time and enhances productivity.

In essence, Copilot Voice represents a leap forward in making AI feel more human. By allowing for smoother, more natural conversations, it removes the barriers that made older AI systems feel mechanical and awkward. It bridges the gap between human communication and AI capabilities, enabling more intuitive, flexible, and efficient interactions that adapt to the needs of the user. With this evolution, Microsoft has successfully addressed the robotic shortcomings of traditional AI, creating an AI companion that feels less like a tool and more like an integral part of the user's daily work and life.

The integration of Copilot Voice into Microsoft's suite of AI tools brings significant benefits to multitasking and overall workflow efficiency. In today's fast-paced work environments, where juggling multiple tasks simultaneously is often necessary, the ability to interact with AI through natural, human-like conversations becomes an invaluable asset. Copilot Voice is designed specifically to support this kind of multitasking, enabling users to manage their workloads more effectively and seamlessly.

One of the key benefits of Copilot Voice for multitasking is its ability to handle tasks without requiring users to stop what they're doing to type out queries or commands. Imagine a scenario where a user is drafting a report while also needing to schedule meetings, check data from spreadsheets, and respond to emails. With traditional AI systems, the user would need to switch between typing out requests or navigating different interfaces, slowing down the overall workflow. However, with Copilot Voice, users can simply speak their requests aloud, allowing the AI to respond in real time. This means that tasks like setting up a meeting, summarizing a document, or pulling information from another file can be done in parallel, without interrupting the primary work at hand.

This hands-free interaction is especially useful for professionals who often find themselves in situations where they cannot easily use a keyboard or mouse. For example, workers in busy office environments, healthcare professionals managing patient records, or financial analysts reviewing multiple sets of data can all benefit from the multitasking capabilities of Copilot Voice. Instead of toggling between tasks, they can verbally command the AI to handle peripheral tasks, enabling them to focus on more critical, strategic activities without losing momentum.

Efficiency is further enhanced by Copilot Voice's **quick response times** and the ability to understand and adapt to the user's workflow. By reducing the lag that is typical in traditional AI systems, Copilot Voice makes it possible for users to keep up their pace without waiting for responses. This is particularly important in work environments where every second counts, such as customer service settings where employees are handling multiple inquiries at once. Copilot Voice allows them to speak naturally, retrieve information quickly, and respond to customers without delays, improving the overall customer experience.

In terms of workflow efficiency, another significant advantage of Copilot Voice is its ability to adapt to non-linear conversations. Workflows are rarely a straight line; they often involve jumping between tasks, revisiting topics, or making real-time adjustments based on new information. Copilot Voice's flexibility allows users to shift from one task to another without losing the thread of the conversation or task at hand. This means that if a user is in the middle of scheduling a meeting but suddenly needs to check the status of a project, Copilot Voice can handle the redirection smoothly and return to the original task when needed. This kind of fluid task-switching is essential for maintaining productivity in dynamic work environments.

The practical value of Copilot Voice extends across various work settings. In **corporate offices**, employees can use it to streamline meetings, manage calendars, and interact with data without leaving their current task. It's particularly valuable in high-pressure settings where speed and accuracy are essential. For **managers**, the ability to verbally instruct Copilot to pull reports, send emails, or arrange team meetings without manually entering commands makes it easier to stay organized while overseeing multiple projects. Copilot Voice acts as a behind-the-scenes assistant, ensuring that administrative tasks are handled quickly so managers can focus on leadership and decision-making.

In **healthcare environments**, the benefits of Copilot Voice are equally profound. Doctors and nurses can use voice commands to update patient records, pull up relevant medical histories, or even receive reminders about upcoming appointments or procedures—all without having to stop and manually enter the data. This hands-free interaction not only saves time but also allows medical professionals to focus more on patient care, knowing that administrative tasks are being managed by an efficient AI partner.

For **creative professionals**, Copilot Voice provides a smoother workflow by handling the logistical aspects of projects. Whether it's organizing files, setting up collaboration spaces, or pulling reference materials, the AI can assist without interrupting the creative process. This allows writers, designers, and artists to stay in the flow of their work without getting bogged down by routine tasks.

In **customer service** and **support roles**, Copilot Voice can be used to quickly access information, retrieve customer data, or draft responses, all while the employee is engaged in a conversation. This real-time assistance reduces wait times for customers and allows employees to focus on providing a personalized experience, rather than spending time searching for information manually.

Overall, Copilot Voice is an essential tool for improving multitasking and workflow efficiency in any setting. Its ability to handle verbal commands, process non-linear tasks, and respond in real time makes it a critical component for anyone looking to streamline their work and maximize productivity. By allowing users to focus on high-value tasks while the AI manages routine ones, Copilot Voice transforms the way people work, ensuring smoother, more efficient operations in any professional environment.

Chapter 5: Copilot Daily: Personalized Briefings at Your Fingertips

Copilot Daily is one of the more personalized features of Microsoft's AI-driven Copilot system, designed to deliver curated information that helps users start their day informed and prepared. At its core, Copilot Daily acts like a digital briefing service, pulling together relevant news, weather updates, and other key information that aligns with each user's individual preferences and routines. Rather than having to sift through multiple apps or websites, users can rely on Copilot Daily to provide a comprehensive snapshot of the day ahead, all in one place.

What makes Copilot Daily stand out is its ability to go beyond delivering generic news or weather updates. It pulls information from trusted sources like **Reuters, The Financial Times, USA Today**, and other reputable outlets to ensure that users receive high-quality, reliable content. By aggregating news from a variety of publishers,

Copilot Daily ensures that the information is well-rounded, offering a diverse perspective on current events, financial updates, and even industry-specific news that could be relevant to the user's work or personal interests.

One of the most appealing aspects of Copilot Daily is how it **curates content** based on individual user preferences. Instead of bombarding users with a long list of headlines or random pieces of information, the AI learns over time what matters most to each person. For instance, if a user consistently shows interest in technology news, financial markets, or local weather, Copilot Daily will prioritize these topics, delivering them front and center. This **tailored experience** adapts over time, ensuring that each user gets the most relevant information to help them start their day efficiently and with purpose.

The system accomplishes this level of personalization by leveraging AI algorithms that track and learn from the user's engagement with content over time. For example, if a user frequently clicks on stories related to a particular industry, Copilot Daily will start to prioritize similar topics in future briefings. It also adjusts the delivery of other types of information, such as weather updates, based on where the user is located and what they typically like to see in their briefings.

Another important aspect of Copilot Daily is its **audio format**, which makes it even more convenient for users who are multitasking or on the go. Whether someone is commuting to work, preparing breakfast, or exercising, they can listen to their personalized briefing without needing to scroll through a screen. This is especially helpful for users who prefer to consume information passively while they complete other tasks, adding to the overall efficiency of their daily routine.

Copilot Daily's value extends to a wide variety of users, from professionals needing quick financial updates before heading into meetings, to individuals who simply want a curated snapshot of the day's events before starting their day. The **partnerships with established news outlets** ensure that the content is reliable and of high quality, allowing users to trust the information they're receiving without having to verify it through multiple sources.

In addition to traditional news, **Copilot Daily also provides updates on other important aspects of daily life**, such as weather forecasts tailored to the user's location, sports scores, and even updates on events or appointments they may have in their calendar. By syncing with Microsoft's ecosystem, Copilot Daily becomes a one-stop hub for essential information, saving users time and helping them prioritize their activities for the day.

This high level of curation reflects Microsoft's commitment to making Copilot Daily a truly personal experience. It's not just about delivering headlines, but about creating a tailored briefing that evolves with the user's habits and interests. Whether someone is interested in international politics, local weather patterns, or updates from specific industries, Copilot Daily ensures they receive the most relevant information without having to wade through unnecessary content.

In summary, **Copilot Daily** serves as a personalized, curated briefing tool, designed to help users stay informed with minimal effort. Its ability to pull trusted news, weather, and updates from various high-quality sources and present them in a format that fits the user's preferences makes it a powerful tool for those looking to start their day efficiently. By tailoring content to individual needs, it enhances productivity and ensures that users have access to the information that matters most to them, wherever they are.

One of the key strengths of Copilot Daily lies in its partnerships with trusted news outlets, such as **Reuters**, **USA Today**, and **The Financial Times**, among others. These partnerships allow Microsoft to deliver reliable and high-quality content to users, ensuring that the information curated for daily briefings is accurate, relevant, and sourced from reputable institutions. By working with such established news providers, Microsoft has positioned Copilot Daily as a dependable source for up-to-date information, allowing users to trust the content they receive without having to double-check its credibility.

These news partnerships also ensure that the breadth of content available to Copilot Daily users covers a wide range of interests and industries. Reuters, for example, is known for its global news coverage, financial insights, and political reporting, making it a valuable source for users interested in international affairs or economic developments. Similarly, USA Today offers broad coverage of national news, lifestyle topics, and breaking stories in the U.S., providing users with a well-rounded view of current events.

By pulling from such diverse and authoritative sources, Copilot Daily can offer users a more complete picture of the day's news, blending in-depth analysis from financial markets with lighter, human-interest stories. This variety ensures that users receive content tailored to both their professional and personal interests, all in one streamlined briefing.

Beyond news, these partnerships extend to other aspects of daily updates. For example, weather reports and sports scores come from trusted providers, ensuring that the briefings include timely, localized, and accurate information. These updates can be crucial for users planning their day, especially those who need to stay informed about weather patterns or traffic conditions before commuting or traveling.

What makes Copilot Daily particularly powerful is its **ability to evolve and personalize over time**. Microsoft has designed the tool to become more finely tuned to each user's preferences, learning from interactions and adapting based on what the user engages with most frequently. This evolving personalization means that Copilot Daily becomes smarter the more it is used, adjusting the content it delivers to align more closely with individual interests and needs.

For instance, if a user consistently clicks on stories about technology and financial markets, Copilot Daily will start to prioritize these topics in future briefings. Over time, it may offer more in-depth coverage of industry-specific news or suggest articles that align with the user's professional focus. Similarly, if a user tends to skip certain types of content, such as entertainment news, the AI will gradually de-emphasize those topics, providing a more tailored experience that reflects the user's unique preferences.

This adaptive learning goes beyond just the types of stories users prefer; it also refines how the content is delivered. For example, if a user frequently listens to their briefings while commuting, Copilot Daily may optimize the format of the updates to be more audio-friendly, offering concise summaries rather than long, detailed reports. On the other hand, for users who engage more deeply with text-based briefings, the AI might suggest more detailed articles or deeper analysis from trusted news outlets.

The personalization aspect of Copilot Daily is continuously improving, allowing users to enjoy a more customized experience that becomes increasingly aligned with their habits and preferences. Over time, the tool is not only a convenient way to stay informed but also a reflection of each user's unique needs and interests, making it an indispensable part of their daily routine.

In summary, the partnerships with trusted news outlets like Reuters and USA Today provide the foundation for the high-quality content delivered through Copilot Daily. As the tool learns from user interactions, it evolves into a highly personalized briefing system, adapting its content to suit individual preferences. This ability to curate and refine information over time, combined with the reliability of its sources, makes Copilot Daily a powerful and trustworthy assistant for staying informed and organized.

Chapter 6: The Hardware Behind Copilot: Co-Pilot Plus PCs

Co-Pilot Plus PCs represent the next step in optimizing AI functionality for users who need high-performance machines capable of seamlessly integrating with Microsoft's advanced AI systems. These PCs are specifically designed to take full advantage of Copilot's features, including its most sophisticated capabilities, ensuring that users experience smooth, uninterrupted performance when engaging with AI tools. Microsoft developed Co-Pilot Plus PCs with the understanding that as AI becomes more integral to productivity and workflow, the hardware that supports these systems must be equally advanced to keep pace with user demands.

What makes Co-Pilot Plus PCs stand out is their ability to handle complex AI-driven tasks, such as real-time data analysis, multitasking across various applications, and managing high volumes of information without slowing down. Built with advanced processors and optimized for AI workloads, these machines allow users to fully harness the power of Copilot without experiencing delays or lag. This is crucial for professionals who rely on AI for decision-making, project management, and other intensive tasks that demand both speed and precision.

One of the standout features of Co-Pilot Plus PCs is **Recall**, a tool designed to help users pick up exactly where they left off in their work. The concept behind Recall is both simple and revolutionary: rather than forcing users to manually re-open documents, applications, or browser tabs after a break or system reboot, Recall remembers the state of your work across apps and automatically restores it. This means users can dive back into their tasks without the usual friction of re-navigating their workspace.

Recall addresses one of the common pain points in modern work environments: the need to juggle multiple tasks, applications, and projects at once. In a typical workflow, users often switch between various programs—such as word processors, spreadsheets, web browsers, and email clients—throughout the day. When a session is interrupted, whether by a system restart, a meeting, or even a quick break, it can be frustrating and time-consuming to reopen each document or re-load each application to continue where things were left off. Recall eliminates this issue by instantly restoring the user's entire workspace to its previous state.

This capability is particularly valuable for professionals who work on long-term, complex projects, such as software developers, graphic designers, and financial analysts. Instead of wasting time reconfiguring their workspace after each interruption, they can rely on Recall to maintain their flow of work, allowing them to resume tasks with minimal disruption. Whether it's reopening design software with the exact files in place or resuming a coding project with all tabs and tools ready, Recall ensures that the user's work environment remains intact.

Moreover, Recall doesn't just apply to one application or a single file—it works across all the tools the user was working with at the time. For example, if someone was drafting a report in Microsoft Word, analyzing data in Excel, and conducting research in a web browser, Recall can reopen all of these programs exactly as they were, allowing for a seamless transition back into the workflow.

Beyond convenience, Recall also improves productivity by minimizing the cognitive load that comes with reorienting oneself after an interruption. This feature allows users to maintain focus and momentum, reducing the friction that typically comes with shifting back into work mode. In fast-paced environments where efficiency is key, such as in tech development, marketing, or finance, this can have a significant impact on overall output.

While the rollout of Recall was initially delayed due to privacy and security concerns, Microsoft has worked diligently to address these issues, ensuring that user data is protected and that sensitive information is not compromised during the process. The feature is now set to be released on Snapdragon-powered PCs first, with Intel and AMD-powered machines following soon after. Once fully deployed, Recall is expected to become a game-changer for users who need reliable, AI-enhanced systems to manage their workloads efficiently.

In summary, Co-Pilot Plus PCs are designed to enhance AI functionality, providing users with the high-performance capabilities needed to fully utilize Copilot's advanced features. The introduction of **Recall** marks a significant improvement in how users manage their tasks, allowing them to pick up where they left off without the usual interruptions or complications. This feature, combined with the power and efficiency of

Co-Pilot Plus PCs, redefines the way users engage with their digital workspaces, streamlining workflows and improving overall productivity.

When Microsoft first developed the **Recall** feature for Co-Pilot Plus PCs, one of the key challenges was addressing privacy concerns and ensuring that user data remained secure. Given that Recall is designed to remember the state of a user's workspace across multiple apps and documents, it involves handling sensitive information that may include personal files, confidential business data, or critical project information. Naturally, there was hesitation around the potential risks of storing or processing this information, especially if it could be accessed or misused during the recall process.

To tackle these concerns, Microsoft implemented robust privacy safeguards to ensure that Recall operates without compromising user data security. One of the first measures Microsoft took was to ensure that Recall does not store information indefinitely or in any unsecured locations. Instead, the data about the user's workspace state is kept locally on the device and is encrypted, making it accessible only when needed and only by the authorized user. This prevents any unauthorized access or breaches during the recall process.

Additionally, Microsoft took time to refine Recall's operational framework to ensure it wouldn't inadvertently compromise privacy. This included designing the system to automatically discard any workspace data once it's no longer needed or once the user logs out of their session. Microsoft also built in user control options, allowing individuals to decide when and how Recall is activated, giving them the flexibility to manage their privacy settings according to their specific needs.

The delay in rolling out Recall was primarily due to the need to balance **usability with data security**. Microsoft understood that while users would benefit greatly from the convenience of instant workspace recovery, it was essential to ensure that these features were airtight in terms of security. The extra time spent fine-tuning the feature before release has paid off, as Recall is now considered a highly secure yet powerful tool for enhancing productivity, with user privacy protected at every step.

Click Todo is another game-changing feature that's part of the Co-Pilot Plus PCs experience, designed to make multitasking even more efficient by offering real-time suggestions based on what the user is currently doing. While Recall helps users pick up where they left off, Click Todo takes it a step further by proactively streamlining their workflow as they work across different tasks.

The essence of Click Todo is that it analyzes the user's activity on their screen and suggests immediate, relevant actions they can take to improve their productivity. For example, if a user is editing a document in Microsoft Word, Click Todo might suggest adding key points from a spreadsheet the user has open in another window. Similarly, if the user is in the middle of preparing a presentation, Click Todo could recommend pulling in images, references, or data from other files they've recently used.

This level of real-time assistance means that users don't have to break their focus to navigate between different tasks manually or search for tools they might need. Instead, Click Todo presents suggestions as a seamless overlay on the screen, allowing users to act on them instantly without interrupting their workflow. This is particularly valuable in fast-paced environments where time is critical, and efficiency is essential.

Click Todo also enhances multitasking by integrating across various Microsoft apps, such as Word, Excel, PowerPoint, and Teams. For instance, if a user is managing a project in Microsoft Teams and simultaneously reviewing progress reports in Excel, Click Todo might suggest scheduling a follow-up meeting or sending a summary to the team based on the current context of the user's work. These intelligent suggestions help users stay on top of tasks without the need to switch between apps or manually input commands.

The goal of Click Todo is to **reduce the cognitive load** associated with multitasking. By offering helpful suggestions at just the right moment, it allows users to focus on the bigger picture while the system handles the smaller, routine tasks in the background. This results in a smoother, more productive workflow, where users can execute multiple tasks without feeling overwhelmed by the complexity of managing them all at once.

In practical terms, Click Todo has been particularly effective in environments where users need to stay organized and efficient under pressure, such as project management, customer service, and data analysis roles. In these fields, professionals are often required to handle multiple streams of information at once, and Click Todo offers the real-time insights and actions they need to stay ahead without getting bogged down by manual processes.

In summary, Microsoft's approach to developing the Recall feature involved prioritizing user privacy and security while enhancing convenience for productivity, resulting in a robust, secure tool for workspace management. Meanwhile, Click Todo takes multitasking to a new level by offering intelligent, real-time suggestions that streamline workflows, allowing users to stay focused and efficient in dynamic work environments. Together, these features make Co-Pilot Plus PCs an essential tool for professionals who demand top-tier AI-enhanced functionality in their daily tasks.

Chapter 7: Windows 11 24H2 Update: Elevating the AI Experience

When Microsoft first developed the **Recall** feature for Co-Pilot Plus PCs, one of the key challenges was addressing privacy concerns and ensuring that user data remained secure. Given that Recall is designed to remember the state of a user's workspace across multiple apps and documents, it involves handling sensitive information that may include personal files, confidential business data, or critical project information. Naturally, there was hesitation around the potential risks of storing or processing this information, especially if it could be accessed or misused during the recall process.

To tackle these concerns, Microsoft implemented robust privacy safeguards to ensure that Recall operates without compromising user data security. One of the first measures Microsoft took was to ensure that Recall does not store information indefinitely or in any unsecured locations. Instead, the data about the user's workspace state is kept locally on the device and is encrypted, making it accessible only when needed and only by the authorized user. This prevents any unauthorized access or breaches during the recall process.

Additionally, Microsoft took time to refine Recall's operational framework to ensure it wouldn't inadvertently compromise privacy. This included designing the system to automatically discard any workspace data once it's no longer needed or once the user logs out of their session. Microsoft also built in user control options, allowing individuals to decide when and how Recall is activated, giving them the flexibility to manage their privacy settings according to their specific needs.

The delay in rolling out Recall was primarily due to the need to balance **usability with data security**. Microsoft understood that while users would benefit greatly from the convenience of instant workspace recovery, it was essential to ensure that these features were airtight in terms of security. The extra time spent fine-tuning the feature before release has paid off, as Recall is now considered a highly secure yet powerful tool for enhancing productivity, with user privacy protected at every step.

Click Todo is another game-changing feature that's part of the Co-Pilot Plus PCs experience, designed to make multitasking even more efficient by offering real-time suggestions based on what the user is currently doing. While Recall helps users pick up where they left off, Click Todo takes it a step further by proactively streamlining their workflow as they work across different tasks.

The essence of Click Todo is that it analyzes the user's activity on their screen and suggests immediate, relevant actions they can take to improve their productivity. For example, if a user is editing a document in Microsoft Word, Click Todo might suggest adding key points from a spreadsheet the user has open in another window. Similarly, if the user is in the middle of preparing a presentation, Click Todo could recommend pulling in images, references, or data from other files they've recently used.

This level of real-time assistance means that users don't have to break their focus to navigate between different tasks manually or search for tools they might need. Instead, Click Todo presents suggestions as a seamless overlay on the screen, allowing users to act on them instantly without interrupting their workflow. This is particularly valuable in fast-paced environments where time is critical, and efficiency is essential.

Click Todo also enhances multitasking by integrating across various Microsoft apps, such as Word, Excel, PowerPoint, and Teams. For instance, if a user is managing a project in Microsoft Teams and simultaneously reviewing progress reports in Excel, Click Todo might suggest scheduling a follow-up meeting or sending a summary to the team based on the current context of the user's work. These intelligent suggestions help users stay on top of tasks without the need to switch between apps or manually input commands.

The goal of Click Todo is to **reduce the cognitive load** associated with multitasking. By offering helpful suggestions at just the right moment, it allows users to focus on the bigger picture while the system handles the smaller, routine tasks in the background. This results in a smoother, more productive workflow, where users can execute multiple tasks without feeling overwhelmed by the complexity of managing them all at once.

In practical terms, Click Todo has been particularly effective in environments where users need to stay organized and efficient under pressure, such as project management, customer service, and data analysis roles. In these fields, professionals are often required to handle multiple streams of information at once, and Click Todo offers the real-time insights and actions they need to stay ahead without getting bogged down by manual processes.

In summary, Microsoft's approach to developing the Recall feature involved prioritizing user privacy and security while enhancing convenience for productivity, resulting in a robust, secure tool for workspace management. Meanwhile, Click Todo takes multitasking to a new level by offering intelligent, real-time suggestions that streamline workflows, allowing users to stay focused and efficient in dynamic work environments. Together, these features make Co-Pilot Plus PCs an essential tool for professionals who demand top-tier AI-enhanced functionality in their daily tasks.

40

You said:

Overview of the 24H2 update and its significance for AI integration. Key features: Wi-Fi 7, HDR backgrounds, and Bluetooth LE audio.

ChatGPT said:

ChatGPT

The **24H2 update** represents a major milestone in Microsoft's journey to integrate artificial intelligence deeper into the Windows operating system. Officially known as **Windows 11 version 24H2**, this update focuses on improving user experience, boosting performance, and enhancing the AI capabilities that are becoming increasingly central to productivity and daily workflows. The update is significant because it builds upon Windows 11's existing AI features, making the operating system smarter, faster, and more responsive to user needs.

At the heart of the 24H2 update is its commitment to seamless **AI integration** across devices, ensuring that AI tools like Copilot are more effectively embedded into the core of the Windows experience. Microsoft is capitalizing on the advancements in machine learning and natural language processing to make AI tools more accessible to everyday users, offering features that can simplify tasks, automate workflows, and provide real-time insights.

The update's AI enhancements don't just apply to Copilot—there's a broad effort to weave AI into nearly every aspect of the system, from system notifications and file management to optimizing performance based on user habits. With 24H2, Microsoft has created an operating system that learns from user interactions, adapting to personal preferences and making AI an integral part of how users engage with their devices. This makes everyday computing more efficient, personalized, and intuitive, which is especially important as AI becomes an indispensable part of both professional and personal digital environments.

In addition to AI improvements, the **24H2 update** introduces several other key features that enhance overall system performance and connectivity:

1. **Wi-Fi 7 Support**:
   One of the most anticipated additions in the

24H2 update is support for **Wi-Fi 7**, the next generation of wireless internet technology. Wi-Fi 7 offers significantly faster data transfer speeds, lower latency, and improved network efficiency, making it ideal for environments where multiple devices are connected to the same network. For users who rely on stable, high-speed internet—whether for gaming, streaming, or remote work—Wi-Fi 7 ensures a smoother, more reliable online experience. This feature is particularly beneficial in settings where large amounts of data need to be transferred quickly or where high-definition video calls and collaboration require seamless connectivity.

2. **HDR Backgrounds**:
   The introduction of **High Dynamic Range (HDR) backgrounds** in the 24H2 update is a visual enhancement that takes advantage of the growing number of HDR-compatible monitors and displays. HDR technology

allows for richer, more vibrant colors, deeper contrasts, and enhanced brightness, creating a more immersive visual experience. With HDR backgrounds, users can enjoy more dynamic and engaging desktop environments, which is not only aesthetically pleasing but also useful for professionals in fields like graphic design, photography, and video editing. This feature highlights Microsoft's commitment to improving both the functionality and the visual appeal of the operating system.

3. **Bluetooth LE Audio**: Another important addition is support for **Bluetooth Low Energy (LE) Audio**, a new standard that improves wireless audio performance. Bluetooth LE Audio is designed to use less power while maintaining high-quality sound, making it ideal for users who frequently use wireless headphones, earbuds, or speakers. This technology also enables features like audio sharing, where

multiple users can connect to the same audio source—a game-changer for collaborative environments or entertainment purposes. Bluetooth LE Audio also supports improved connectivity for assistive hearing devices, broadening accessibility for users who rely on wireless technology for enhanced sound quality.

These key features, along with the broader AI integration, make the 24H2 update an essential upgrade for users looking to stay on the cutting edge of technology. The update not only provides significant performance boosts but also enhances user experience through better connectivity, stunning visuals, and smarter, more adaptive systems. For professionals and casual users alike, 24H2 represents a leap forward in making Windows 11 a more intelligent, versatile platform that adapts to the demands of modern computing.

In summary, the **24H2 update** is a critical step in Microsoft's efforts to enhance AI integration within its operating system, making AI tools more accessible and useful for a wider range of tasks. At the same time, features like Wi-Fi 7 support, HDR backgrounds, and Bluetooth LE Audio ensure that the update brings tangible improvements to performance, connectivity, and user experience, solidifying Windows 11 as a future-ready platform for both work and play.

The **24H2 update** also brings exciting enhancements to some of Microsoft's most essential apps, including **Photos** and **Paint**, with a focus on leveraging AI to improve usability and functionality. These updates reflect Microsoft's broader AI vision of embedding intelligent features throughout the user experience, making everyday tasks easier, faster, and more creative.

In the **Photos** app, one of the standout updates is the introduction of **super resolution**, which allows users to upscale image quality with a single click. Powered by AI, this feature enhances the resolution of low-quality images, sharpening details and making pictures clearer and more vibrant. This is particularly useful for users working with older or low-resolution images that may need to be repurposed for modern projects. Whether you're a casual user looking to improve your personal photos or a professional who needs higher-quality images for presentations or design work, this AI-driven feature offers significant improvements without the need for advanced editing skills.

The **Paint** app also receives a major update in the 24H2 version, incorporating new **AI-powered features** like **generative fill** and **erase**. These tools make it easier than ever to modify and enhance images directly within the app. With generative fill, users can add missing elements or create entire sections of an image using AI-based predictions, which is ideal for filling in gaps in design projects or creating more cohesive visuals. The erase tool allows users to remove unwanted objects or imperfections from an image with precision, using AI to automatically adjust the surrounding area so that the edit blends seamlessly into the background. These features, which were previously reserved for more advanced software like Photoshop, make Paint a more powerful and accessible tool for both casual users and creative professionals.

Beyond these two flagship apps, other essential Microsoft tools also see improvements that streamline user workflows and incorporate more intelligent, responsive features. The **Snipping Tool**, for example, is enhanced with smarter capture options and editing capabilities, while **Notepad** and **File Explorer** gain AI-driven search functions that make finding files and information quicker and more intuitive. These enhancements demonstrate Microsoft's ongoing commitment to embedding AI in ways that meaningfully enhance the user experience across all its core applications.

The updates to Photos, Paint, and other apps represent a larger effort by Microsoft to integrate AI into everyday tasks, transforming routine activities like photo editing, note-taking, and file management into more efficient, enjoyable experiences. These improvements reflect how Microsoft's AI vision isn't just about groundbreaking innovations but also about making even the simplest tools smarter and more useful for everyone.

This AI-driven approach aligns perfectly with Microsoft's broader vision of **integrating AI into every corner of its ecosystem**, turning routine tasks into intelligent processes that save time and increase productivity. The 24H2 update is a clear example of this philosophy in action, as it adds layers of intelligence to the tools users interact with daily, making them more adaptive and capable. The aim is to eliminate the friction points in everyday workflows, enabling users to focus more on creativity and problem-solving, with the AI handling the repetitive or technically complex tasks in the background.

Moreover, this update fits into Microsoft's wider ambition of creating an **AI-first future**, where every device, app, and service leverages AI to enhance productivity, creativity, and convenience. From smart photo editing in Photos to predictive tools in Paint, AI is no longer a luxury feature—it's becoming a standard part of the digital workspace. By embedding AI deeply into Windows and its core applications, Microsoft is ensuring that users have access to powerful, yet intuitive tools that help them work smarter, not harder.

These improvements also showcase Microsoft's **democratization of AI**—making advanced AI tools accessible to everyday users without requiring specialized skills or knowledge. The company's vision is not just about pushing technological boundaries for enterprises or tech enthusiasts but making sure that AI benefits everyone, from casual users to professionals across various industries. The updates introduced in the 24H2 version demonstrate how AI can simplify tasks, spark creativity, and enhance productivity in ways that are both practical and impactful.

In conclusion, the 24H2 update brings significant enhancements to Microsoft's essential apps like Photos and Paint, integrating AI in ways that boost functionality and usability. These improvements are part of Microsoft's broader AI vision, which focuses on embedding intelligent features across its ecosystem, making everyday tasks faster, smarter, and more enjoyable for all users. By continuing to integrate AI into the core of Windows, Microsoft is transforming how people work, create, and interact with technology, shaping a future where AI becomes an invisible yet indispensable part of the user experience.

Chapter 8: Privacy and Security: Microsoft's Commitment

The rise of AI technology has brought about a new set of privacy challenges, as companies and users must balance the incredible utility of AI with the need to maintain strict security and protect personal data. AI systems, like Microsoft's Copilot, are capable of analyzing vast amounts of data, understanding user behavior, and providing tailored responses that enhance productivity. However, these capabilities also raise concerns about how personal information is processed, stored, and safeguarded. To address these privacy challenges, Microsoft has taken proactive steps to ensure that Copilot adheres to stringent privacy protocols without compromising the effectiveness of its AI-driven features.

One of the fundamental privacy challenges in AI is the issue of **data collection and processing**. For AI systems to be useful, they need access to data, which often includes sensitive personal or business information. The dilemma lies in how to give AI the information it needs to perform effectively while ensuring that this data is protected from unauthorized access or misuse. AI systems are often viewed with suspicion because of their ability to analyze personal interactions, habits, and workflows, leading to concerns about potential privacy breaches or data leaks.

To tackle these challenges, Microsoft has implemented several layers of privacy protection in Copilot. First and foremost, the company has built Copilot to be **transparent and user-controlled**, meaning that users are always in charge of what data is accessed and how it is used. For instance, many of Copilot's advanced features, like **Copilot Vision**, are opt-in, giving users full control over when and how the AI can analyze their screen or interact with their documents. This prevents any unauthorized use of data and ensures that users actively choose when to engage the AI's more advanced capabilities.

Microsoft also adheres to a **data minimization** principle, meaning that Copilot collects only the data it absolutely needs to perform its tasks. This approach significantly reduces the risk of excessive data collection or misuse. Furthermore, the data that is processed by Copilot is either **kept locally on the device** or encrypted before it is transmitted to ensure that no personal or sensitive information is left vulnerable to external threats. By limiting the amount of data Copilot accesses and ensuring that it is securely stored, Microsoft reduces the potential risks associated with AI-driven data analysis.

A major aspect of Copilot's privacy protection lies in **end-to-end encryption**, which ensures that any data exchanged between the user's device and Microsoft's servers is secure. Whether it's personal documents, business emails, or application settings, all information processed by Copilot is encrypted both during transmission and while stored, ensuring that only authorized users and systems can access the data. Additionally, **data**

anonymization techniques are used when necessary, which strips identifying information from user data before it is processed, further enhancing privacy.

Another important privacy feature is that **no data is stored permanently** within Copilot's memory. For example, Copilot Vision's ability to analyze a user's screen is temporary, with all session data being discarded as soon as the user finishes using the feature. This practice prevents any long-term storage of personal information and ensures that sensitive data is not inadvertently used for future AI training or analytics. The strict session-based approach to data handling means that Copilot only holds onto the information it needs for as long as the session is active, after which it is permanently deleted.

Microsoft's **commitment to privacy also extends to compliance with global privacy regulations**, such as the General Data Protection Regulation (GDPR) in Europe. Copilot's features are designed to meet or exceed these privacy standards, ensuring that users around the world can trust the system to respect their rights and protect their personal information. By embedding these regulations into the design and function of Copilot, Microsoft ensures that privacy is not an afterthought, but a foundational element of its AI systems.

Moreover, users have access to **privacy dashboards** that provide insights into what data is being used and how. These dashboards allow users to adjust their privacy settings, manage permissions, and even view logs of past interactions to ensure transparency. This level of control not only increases user confidence but also ensures that Copilot's operation is fully aligned with individual privacy preferences.

In conclusion, Microsoft has faced the privacy challenges of AI head-on by creating a system where the **balance between utility and security** is prioritized. Copilot's advanced AI features are built on a foundation of transparency, user control, encryption, and compliance with international privacy standards. By ensuring that its AI-driven tools adhere to strict privacy protocols, Microsoft has managed to deliver the utility of AI without compromising user trust or the security of personal data. This thoughtful approach allows users to harness the power of Copilot while staying confident that their privacy is protected.

Microsoft's **opt-in** approach and strong focus on **user control** are central to ensuring that its AI tools, like Copilot, operate without compromising privacy or engaging in unwanted surveillance. As AI systems become increasingly integrated into daily life and work, the line between useful assistance and potential privacy invasion can become blurred. Microsoft addresses this concern by giving users the power to decide when and how Copilot interacts with their data, ensuring that AI tools enhance productivity without overstepping personal boundaries.

One of the most significant ways Microsoft achieves this is by making features like **Copilot Vision** entirely opt-in. This means that Copilot only engages with the user's screen or documents when the user actively chooses to enable it. There's no passive monitoring or analysis happening behind the scenes—users maintain control over when the AI is allowed to assist with specific tasks. For example, if a user wants Copilot to analyze a document they're working on or suggest improvements to a presentation, they must explicitly turn the feature on. Once the task is complete, the AI disengages, and no further analysis takes place unless the user chooses to activate it again.

Additionally, Microsoft has implemented **clear notifications and indicators** to ensure that users always know when Copilot's features are active. This transparency is crucial to building trust, as it ensures that users are never unknowingly subjected to surveillance or data analysis. If a feature like Copilot Vision is enabled, users receive visual cues, such as icons or prompts, that make it clear when the AI is processing information. This gives users peace of mind, knowing that they are in control of how and when their data is being used.

Microsoft also offers comprehensive **privacy settings and control panels**, allowing users to manage their data permissions at a granular level. Through these settings, users can customize their AI experience, choosing which types of data Copilot can access and how it interacts with their workflows. These dashboards also allow users to review past interactions with the AI, providing further transparency and control over the information Copilot has processed. If users ever feel that a particular feature oversteps their privacy boundaries, they can easily disable it, reinforcing Microsoft's commitment to user autonomy.

Looking ahead, **privacy will continue to play a pivotal role in shaping the AI landscape**. As AI technology advances, it will become increasingly important to find ways to balance the enormous potential of AI with the need to protect individual rights and personal data. Microsoft's approach to privacy—built on transparency, user control, and consent—will likely become a model for other tech companies as AI tools become more integrated into everyday life.

One key area where privacy will shape the future of AI is in the development of **context-aware systems**. These systems, like Copilot, are designed to understand and respond to user needs in real-time, often by accessing a broad range of personal data. The challenge will be ensuring that such systems can operate effectively while still respecting user privacy. In the future, more sophisticated **privacy-preserving technologies**, such as **differential privacy** and **federated learning**, may be deployed to allow AI systems to learn from data without directly accessing sensitive information. These technologies enable AI to analyze data patterns across many devices without ever accessing individual datasets, which could help alleviate concerns about unwanted surveillance.

Moreover, the evolution of **AI regulations and privacy standards** will play a critical role in defining the future AI landscape. As governments and regulatory bodies introduce new laws around data privacy, companies will need to adapt their AI systems to comply with increasingly stringent requirements. This will likely lead to the development of even more robust privacy features in AI tools, as companies work to meet the expectations of both users and regulators. Microsoft's leadership in adhering to international standards like the **General Data Protection Regulation (GDPR)** sets a strong precedent for how AI companies can balance innovation with privacy protection.

User-centric AI is another future direction where privacy will remain a core focus. As AI systems become more personalized and integrated into various aspects of life—from health and finance to entertainment and communication—users will demand greater control over how their data is used. The ability to tailor privacy settings to fit individual needs will become a standard feature in AI tools, allowing users to dictate the terms of their engagement with AI systems while still benefiting from personalized assistance.

Lastly, the role of **trust** will be essential in determining how widely AI is adopted in the future. Users must feel confident that AI systems are not compromising their privacy or subjecting them to unnecessary surveillance. Companies like Microsoft, which prioritize opt-in features and clear user controls, will set the bar for how AI should operate in a way that respects user autonomy. This emphasis on trust will be a key differentiator for AI systems in a world where privacy concerns continue to grow alongside technological capabilities.

In conclusion, Microsoft's opt-in approach and emphasis on user control provide a robust framework for protecting privacy in the AI-driven future. By ensuring that no unwanted surveillance takes place and that users are always aware of and in control of their data, Microsoft sets an important example for how AI systems should function. Looking ahead, privacy will remain central to the development of AI, influencing everything from regulatory standards to technological innovations. As AI tools become more sophisticated and ubiquitous, maintaining a balance between utility and privacy will be key to fostering trust and ensuring widespread adoption of AI technologies.

Chapter 9: Microsoft's AI Ecosystem: The Power of Integration

Microsoft's competitive edge in the rapidly evolving AI landscape comes from its ability to **integrate Copilot seamlessly across multiple platforms**, including **Windows, Microsoft Edge, and Microsoft Office**. This integration sets Microsoft apart by creating a unified experience for users, allowing them to access AI-driven assistance across the tools they already use every day. Whether you're drafting a document in Word, browsing the web in Edge, or organizing your tasks in Windows, Copilot is embedded into the very core of these platforms, enabling a smooth, continuous interaction with AI across different environments.

One of the most powerful aspects of Copilot's integration is that it works **natively across Windows**, making it accessible directly from the desktop and taskbar. Users can launch Copilot with a single click, bringing AI-powered assistance into any task they're working on without having to switch apps or navigate complicated menus. For instance, if you're working on a presentation in PowerPoint and need help pulling data from Excel, Copilot can handle the task within seconds, extracting relevant information and formatting it appropriately for your slides, all from within the same interface.

The seamless integration extends into **Microsoft Edge**, where Copilot becomes a smart assistant for web browsing. Whether you're conducting research, reading an article, or shopping online, Copilot can interact with the content you're viewing, offering context-aware suggestions and insights. For example, if you're reading a report online, Copilot can summarize key points, provide definitions for technical terms, or even suggest related sources of information without disrupting your browsing experience. This deep integration transforms Microsoft Edge from a standard web browser into an intelligent, interactive tool that boosts productivity by anticipating and assisting with user needs in real time.

The same level of integration is seen across **Microsoft Office**, where Copilot enhances productivity in apps like **Word**, **Excel**, and **Outlook**. In Word, Copilot can help draft documents, summarize long reports, or even suggest edits based on the context of your writing. In Excel, it can analyze complex data sets, create charts, and provide insights that would normally require advanced spreadsheet knowledge. In Outlook, Copilot assists with organizing emails, managing appointments, and even drafting replies based on the tone and content of received messages. This level of integration ensures that AI is not just a separate tool but is embedded within the very functions of these apps, making it easier for users to work efficiently without the need to learn new software or switch between different tools.

What makes Microsoft's approach so effective is the **seamless user experience across platforms**. Because Copilot is integrated directly into the infrastructure of Windows, Edge, and Office, users can move between apps and platforms without having to re-engage or reconfigure the AI. For instance, if a user starts drafting an email in Outlook and needs to reference a document in Word, they can seamlessly transition between the two apps, with Copilot keeping track of the user's workflow and offering assistance relevant to both tasks. This cross-platform capability ensures that the AI is consistently available wherever the user goes, creating a cohesive, uninterrupted workflow.

This **cross-platform integration** is particularly valuable in today's work environments, where users often switch between different tasks and applications throughout the day. Whether it's collaborating with a team via **Microsoft Teams**, organizing tasks in **OneNote**, or conducting research in Edge, Copilot is designed to offer continuous, contextual assistance, reducing the time and effort required to complete tasks. Users don't have to worry about transferring information manually from one app to another; Copilot is always present, ready to assist with whatever the next task requires.

Moreover, Microsoft's ability to integrate Copilot into its ecosystem gives it a unique competitive advantage because it leverages the company's already extensive user base. Millions of users rely on Microsoft's products daily, from individuals using Windows at home to enterprises running Office across entire organizations. By embedding AI into these platforms, Microsoft makes it easy for users to adopt AI tools without needing to transition to a new system or learn a new interface. This seamless integration provides Microsoft with an edge over competitors, as it can introduce advanced AI functionality into the workflows that users are already familiar with.

Another key advantage of this integration is the **synchronization of data and preferences across platforms**. Whether a user is working on a desktop PC at the office, a laptop at home, or a mobile device on the go, Copilot can sync with their Microsoft account to provide a consistent experience. For example, a user's preferences, saved projects, and even AI-generated suggestions can follow them across devices, allowing for a more personalized and efficient experience. This ability to carry over tasks and AI insights across platforms without interruption is a major benefit for professionals who need flexibility and mobility in their work.

Ultimately, Microsoft's strategy of integrating Copilot across Windows, Edge, and Office not only enhances productivity but also reinforces its position as a leader in the AI space. By embedding AI deeply into its ecosystem, Microsoft provides users with a more intelligent, efficient, and user-friendly experience that spans all the platforms they rely on. This holistic approach to AI integration creates a **seamless user experience** that boosts productivity and sets Microsoft apart from competitors who are still working to incorporate AI into their systems in such an effective and cohesive way.

In conclusion, Microsoft's **competitive edge** lies in its ability to make Copilot an integral part of its ecosystem, providing a **seamless experience across Windows, Edge, and Office**. The cross-platform integration ensures that users can rely on AI assistance across multiple environments without disruption, significantly improving workflow efficiency and productivity. This strategic integration not only enhances the capabilities of individual apps but also creates a unified, intelligent user experience that is difficult for competitors to match.

Microsoft's success in the AI space is not just a product of its own internal innovation but also the result of strategic partnerships with some of the most prominent tech companies in the world. These collaborations have allowed Microsoft to leverage the strengths of its partners, expanding the reach and functionality of its AI systems in ways that set it apart from its competitors. One of the most prominent partnerships is with OpenAI, the organization behind breakthrough technologies like GPT (Generative Pre-trained Transformer). By integrating OpenAI's large language models into Microsoft's platforms, such as Azure and Copilot, Microsoft has significantly enhanced its AI capabilities, particularly in the areas of natural language processing and machine learning. This partnership has made Microsoft's AI tools some of the most advanced in the industry, capable of understanding and responding to user inputs in a more human-like and nuanced way.

The collaboration with OpenAI is just one example of how Microsoft has strategically aligned itself with innovators in AI. Another key partnership is with NVIDIA, whose cutting-edge graphics processing units (GPUs) provide the backbone for many of Microsoft's AI-driven tasks. By utilizing NVIDIA's technology, Microsoft ensures that its AI systems are capable of handling the immense computational workloads required for tasks like real-time data analysis, complex simulations, and large-scale machine learning. This alliance allows Microsoft's AI systems to operate faster and more efficiently, providing a smoother user experience while also delivering the power needed for businesses and developers to run AI models at scale.

Beyond OpenAI and NVIDIA, Microsoft has formed alliances with companies like LinkedIn, Adobe, and SAP, further expanding the practical applications of its AI technologies. With LinkedIn, Microsoft has integrated AI-driven insights into professional networking and recruitment, providing more intelligent job recommendations, improved candidate matching, and deeper workforce analytics. This integration highlights how Microsoft's AI isn't just about automating tasks but about creating smarter, more personalized experiences across industries.

In Adobe's case, the partnership enables Microsoft to bring AI into creative workflows. By integrating Adobe's creative software with Microsoft's AI systems, professionals can use tools that help automate design processes, enhance visual content, and streamline creative tasks. For businesses, the collaboration with SAP allows Microsoft to incorporate AI into enterprise solutions like supply chain management and customer relationship management, helping companies make more informed decisions based on real-time data insights. These partnerships demonstrate that Microsoft's AI strategy is not just about making its own tools better but about creating a broader ecosystem where AI enhances functionality across a variety of platforms and industries.

Looking ahead, Microsoft's vision for AI integration will only deepen as the technology continues to evolve. AI is already embedded in many aspects of

Microsoft's offerings, from cloud computing with Azure to productivity tools like Microsoft 365, but the future promises even more advanced and seamless integration. AI will continue to become more intuitive and context-aware, further blending into the fabric of everyday tasks without requiring users to engage with it directly. Instead of relying on manual inputs, future AI systems will anticipate user needs, learning from behavior patterns and providing intelligent assistance before a command is even issued. This shift toward proactive AI is central to Microsoft's long-term strategy, ensuring that its technology remains not only powerful but also highly user-friendly.

One of the key areas where AI will have a growing presence is within Microsoft's suite of productivity tools. Already, Copilot enhances applications like Word, Excel, and PowerPoint by providing intelligent suggestions, generating content, and assisting with data analysis. Over time, these features will evolve into even more sophisticated systems that can predict what users need based on their workflow. For instance, AI could suggest the best way to visualize complex data in Excel or recommend edits to a document in Word based on the user's writing style and previous work. This kind of predictive AI will make Microsoft's tools more efficient and tailored to individual user preferences, transforming how people work on a daily basis.

AI will also continue to revolutionize the way businesses operate by enhancing decision-making processes. In sectors like finance, healthcare, and retail, AI-powered analytics will enable companies to analyze vast amounts of data in real-time, uncovering patterns and trends that were previously difficult to detect. Microsoft's enterprise solutions, such as Dynamics 365, will incorporate these capabilities, allowing businesses to gain insights that improve operations, enhance customer experiences, and drive growth. AI will no longer be just an added feature but a core component of how organizations function, helping them stay competitive in an increasingly data-driven world.

Microsoft's focus on privacy and ethical AI development will remain central as it moves forward. As AI becomes more deeply integrated into every aspect of technology, ensuring that these systems are transparent, accountable, and fair will be critical. Microsoft's commitment to responsible AI development means that future iterations of its tools will continue to prioritize user control and data security, ensuring that AI works in ways that respect individual privacy and protect sensitive information.

In summary, Microsoft's ability to stand out in the AI landscape stems from its strategic partnerships with industry leaders like OpenAI, NVIDIA, and Adobe. These collaborations have allowed Microsoft to create a robust and versatile AI ecosystem that enhances its own tools while integrating seamlessly with those from other companies. As AI continues to evolve, it will become even more embedded in

Microsoft's offerings, transforming how individuals and businesses interact with technology. The future of AI at Microsoft is one of deeper integration, enhanced predictive capabilities, and a continued focus on ethical, user-friendly design.

Chapter 10: The Future of AI with Microsoft Copilot

As Microsoft continues to innovate and expand the capabilities of Copilot, the next phase of its evolution is poised to bring even greater levels of intelligence, personalization, and seamless integration across industries. One of the key predictions for the next phase of Copilot involves its increasing ability to anticipate user needs and offer proactive assistance, rather than simply reacting to user commands. This shift will see Copilot move from being a tool that responds to inputs into a system that learns from user behavior, identifies patterns, and offers suggestions or solutions before users even realize they need them.

In this next phase, Copilot will become even more contextually aware. For example, if a user is drafting an email, Copilot may suggest relevant attachments based on previous conversations, or it might preemptively flag important calendar events that are related to the content being written. In more complex tasks, such as financial analysis or project management, Copilot will be able to offer predictive insights based on data trends, helping users make informed decisions faster and more effectively. This ability to "read between the lines" will set Copilot apart, making it an indispensable tool in both professional and personal settings.

Moreover, the integration of **multimodal capabilities** is expected to enhance Copilot's flexibility. This means that Copilot will not only respond to text commands but will also interpret visual data, such as graphs, images, or video content, providing real-time analysis and feedback across a variety of media. For example, if a user is working on a presentation in PowerPoint, Copilot could analyze the visual structure of the slides, suggesting layout improvements or generating relevant graphics based on the content. In industries like design, marketing, and media production, this multimodal functionality will significantly streamline workflows, enhancing creative output while saving time.

Another exciting development is the potential for **cross-platform continuity**, allowing Copilot to follow users across devices and applications without losing context. Imagine beginning a task on a desktop at work, then continuing it seamlessly on a mobile device or tablet while on the go, with Copilot retaining full awareness of the task's history, associated files, and next steps. This cross-platform fluidity will be key in an increasingly mobile and remote work environment, where users need their tools to be accessible anytime and anywhere, without interruptions or loss of data.

A critical aspect of the next phase of Copilot is its **human-centric approach**, which is expected to transform industries by reshaping the way people interact with technology. This approach focuses on making AI more intuitive, personal, and adaptable to human needs, ultimately improving the user experience in meaningful ways. By enhancing user engagement, Copilot's human-centric design will drive productivity, creativity, and decision-making across a wide range of sectors.

In **healthcare**, for instance, Copilot's ability to analyze patient data and provide insights will aid doctors in developing personalized treatment plans, reducing administrative burdens, and ensuring that healthcare professionals have access to the most up-to-date information. By improving efficiency in diagnostics and treatment recommendations, Copilot will help healthcare systems deliver better patient outcomes, streamline operations, and reduce costs.

In **education**, Copilot can act as a virtual tutor or assistant for both teachers and students. For students, Copilot can help in learning by offering personalized study plans, analyzing academic performance, and providing targeted support in areas where they may be struggling. For educators, Copilot can automate grading, track student progress, and even suggest curriculum adjustments based on the needs of individual students or classes. This human-centric AI approach will make learning more tailored and effective, creating a more supportive environment for both teaching and studying.

In the **financial sector**, Copilot will offer predictive analytics to assist businesses and individuals with investment decisions, financial planning, and risk assessment. By analyzing trends in real-time and providing insights based on historical data, Copilot will help financial advisors and business leaders make more informed decisions. In this context, AI-driven tools like Copilot will not only enhance productivity but also drive smarter, more strategic financial management.

In **manufacturing and logistics**, Copilot's human-centric AI will enhance operational efficiency by optimizing supply chains, predicting equipment maintenance needs, and streamlining production schedules. The predictive capabilities of

Copilot will allow businesses to minimize downtime, reduce waste, and respond more agilely to market demand. This will lead to significant cost savings and improvements in overall efficiency, helping industries adapt to rapidly changing global markets.

In **customer service and sales**, Copilot's next phase will enable more personalized, data-driven interactions between businesses and their customers. AI-driven insights will allow customer service representatives to respond more effectively to inquiries, offering solutions based on past interactions and preferences. In sales, Copilot will assist in generating leads, managing client relationships, and tailoring pitches to individual customers, ultimately enhancing customer satisfaction and driving revenue growth.

At the core of these transformations is the concept of **augmenting human capabilities**, rather than replacing them. Copilot's human-centric approach is designed to empower individuals, helping them achieve more by reducing the cognitive load of routine tasks and providing intelligent, context-aware assistance. Whether in a professional setting, such as managing complex business operations, or in personal productivity tasks like organizing a schedule, Copilot's intuitive, user-focused design will create a more efficient and rewarding experience.

Looking further into the future, we can expect Copilot to integrate even more **deep learning** techniques, allowing it to better understand human emotions, preferences, and communication styles. This could lead to AI systems that can interact in more empathetic, nuanced ways, adapting their responses based on the emotional tone or stress levels of the user. For instance, in high-pressure environments like emergency response teams or legal consultations, AI systems like Copilot could detect the urgency of the situation and adjust their behavior accordingly, offering more streamlined or simplified information to reduce stress and improve decision-making.

In conclusion, the next phase of Copilot will see it evolve from a responsive assistant to a proactive, context-aware partner that anticipates user needs and enhances productivity across industries. Its human-centric approach will transform how businesses and individuals interact with AI, offering more personalized, seamless, and intelligent support in various professional environments. By empowering users with AI-driven insights and tools, Copilot is set to drive the next wave of innovation, productivity, and human-AI collaboration.

As artificial intelligence continues to advance, its influence is expanding far beyond the realms of productivity and business efficiency. AI is increasingly becoming a transformative force in critical sectors such as **education**, **healthcare**, and **beyond**, reshaping how people learn, how healthcare is delivered, and even how societies function. Microsoft's role in this AI revolution has been pivotal, as it not only provides cutting-edge AI tools but also drives innovation that addresses real-world challenges, ensuring that AI's benefits reach diverse sectors in ways that truly improve lives.

In **education**, AI is rapidly changing the landscape of how students learn and how teachers instruct. Traditionally, learning has been a one-size-fits-all model, where the pace and content of instruction are fixed for all students, regardless of their individual needs or abilities. AI is altering this by enabling **personalized learning experiences** tailored to the needs of each student. With tools like Copilot, Microsoft is helping educators develop adaptive learning systems that can assess students' strengths and weaknesses in real-time. This allows teachers to offer targeted support where students struggle, ensuring that no one is left behind. AI-powered platforms can also automate grading, create customized lesson plans, and provide instant feedback on assignments, making the learning process more efficient and tailored.

For students, AI brings interactive, intuitive learning experiences to life. Imagine an AI tutor available 24/7, helping students with difficult subjects by offering additional resources, explaining concepts in different ways, and even adjusting learning strategies based on individual performance. Microsoft's AI technologies facilitate these experiences, giving students the support they need to excel in their studies. This personalized, flexible approach to education will become even more prominent in the future, bridging the gap between different learning styles and ensuring that education is more inclusive and accessible.

Healthcare is another area where AI's role is growing significantly, with transformative potential that is already being realized. The medical field generates an immense amount of data every day, from patient records and lab results to clinical trials and imaging data. AI's ability to process and analyze this data in real-time allows for faster, more accurate diagnoses, improved patient care, and more effective treatments. Microsoft's AI-driven tools are at the forefront of this revolution, enabling healthcare providers to make better-informed decisions.

One of the most promising applications of AI in healthcare is in **predictive analytics**, which helps doctors and healthcare professionals anticipate health issues before they become critical. AI can analyze a patient's medical history, lifestyle, and genetic data to predict the likelihood of certain diseases, enabling earlier interventions and more personalized treatments. Microsoft's **Azure AI** plays a key role in supporting healthcare providers with scalable AI infrastructure that can handle these vast datasets, helping medical professionals make quicker, more accurate diagnoses and treatment plans.

Beyond diagnostics, AI is also playing a key role in areas like **medical research** and **drug**

discovery. Microsoft's AI tools are helping researchers accelerate the development of new treatments by analyzing massive amounts of clinical data to identify patterns and potential therapeutic targets. This has the potential to shorten the time it takes to bring life-saving drugs to market, revolutionizing how medical research is conducted. Additionally, AI-driven robotics and automation are enhancing precision in surgeries and other medical procedures, further advancing healthcare outcomes.

Outside of education and healthcare, AI is playing a critical role in **industries like agriculture, environmental sustainability, and public services**. In agriculture, AI systems analyze weather patterns, soil conditions, and crop data to optimize planting schedules, reduce water usage, and improve yields. By integrating AI with **IoT (Internet of Things)** devices, farmers can monitor crops in real-time and take proactive measures to protect against pests or droughts.

Microsoft's Azure platform provides the infrastructure for these AI-powered agricultural tools, contributing to smarter, more sustainable farming practices.

In the **environmental sustainability** sector, AI is helping to monitor climate change, predict natural disasters, and manage energy consumption. By analyzing data from satellites, sensors, and other monitoring systems, AI can predict shifts in climate patterns, helping governments and organizations take preemptive action. Additionally, AI tools are being used to optimize energy usage in buildings, reducing waste and promoting green energy solutions. Microsoft's commitment to sustainability includes using AI to drive innovations in environmental protection, ensuring that technology plays a role in safeguarding the planet for future generations.

Public services and **government operations** are also benefiting from AI's capabilities. In smart cities, AI is being used to optimize traffic flow, manage public transportation, and improve emergency response times. Microsoft's AI platforms provide the backbone for many of these systems, enabling governments to make data-driven decisions that enhance public safety and quality of life. By automating repetitive administrative tasks, AI is also helping government agencies reduce bureaucratic inefficiencies and deliver services more effectively.

Microsoft has been instrumental in **shaping the AI revolution**, not just by developing advanced AI tools but also by promoting ethical and responsible AI usage. One of the company's core missions has been to ensure that AI is designed with human needs at the forefront, promoting inclusivity, privacy, and fairness in AI applications. Microsoft has consistently advocated for **ethical AI principles**, ensuring that the technology is used in ways that benefit society rather than exacerbating existing inequalities.

The company's **responsible AI framework** emphasizes transparency, accountability, and fairness. Microsoft is committed to building AI systems that users can trust, ensuring that AI operates in a way that respects privacy and mitigates bias. Through partnerships with academic institutions, governments, and non-profits, Microsoft is working to create a world where AI benefits all sectors of society, from education and healthcare to the environment and public services.

As AI continues to evolve, Microsoft will remain at the forefront of driving these advancements. The company's strategic vision involves not only improving the capabilities of AI but also ensuring that it is used to solve the world's most pressing challenges. By integrating AI into every facet of its offerings, from productivity tools to enterprise solutions, Microsoft is setting the stage for a future where AI is an integral part of everyday life, enhancing human potential and creating a more connected, efficient, and equitable world.

In conclusion, AI's role is growing far beyond productivity tools, transforming education, healthcare, and industries like agriculture and public services. Microsoft's leadership in the AI revolution is clear as it continues to push the boundaries of what AI can achieve, while ensuring that this powerful technology is used ethically and responsibly. The future of AI, driven by Microsoft's innovations, promises to reshape how we learn, how we heal, and how we build a sustainable future for generations to come.

Conclusion

As we reflect on the journey of Copilot and its transformative role in reshaping productivity and human interaction, it becomes clear that Microsoft has positioned itself at the forefront of the AI revolution. Copilot is no longer just an intelligent assistant that helps with mundane tasks—it is a game-changer that seamlessly integrates into the workflow of users, adapting to their needs and delivering real-time, context-aware assistance. From its ability to provide personalized recommendations in Office applications to its capability to handle complex data analysis and automate routine processes, Copilot has evolved into a sophisticated tool that empowers users across industries. Its features, such as predictive insights, real-time collaboration tools, and advanced natural language processing, have made it a vital partner in day-to-day operations.

The broader impact of AI on productivity and human interaction extends far beyond just convenience. AI's integration into daily work processes has opened up new possibilities for efficiency, creativity, and collaboration. By automating repetitive tasks, offering data-driven insights, and enhancing decision-making, AI allows professionals to focus on higher-level strategic thinking. Moreover, as AI tools become more intuitive and human-centric, they foster a more seamless interaction between humans and technology, transforming how people communicate, work, and solve problems. The rise of Copilot and other AI systems signals a future where technology anticipates user needs, adapts to individual work styles, and offers proactive solutions that elevate productivity and creativity to new heights.

At the core of Microsoft's AI strategy is its unwavering commitment to **privacy** and **innovation**. Throughout the development of Copilot and its other AI offerings, Microsoft has prioritized user control, ensuring that privacy is never compromised. The opt-in nature of advanced features, along with strong data encryption and ethical AI practices, reflects Microsoft's dedication to building tools that users can trust. By putting privacy at the forefront, Microsoft has created AI systems that are both powerful and secure, giving users confidence that their personal information is protected. This balance of privacy and utility ensures that AI can be leveraged effectively while respecting the boundaries of user data.

As the world continues to embrace AI, Microsoft's **commitment to innovation** is evident in its forward-thinking approach to AI integration. From partnerships with tech leaders like OpenAI and NVIDIA to driving advancements in education, healthcare, and enterprise solutions, Microsoft is continuously pushing the boundaries of what AI can achieve. Its vision of a future where AI is embedded in every aspect of technology—helping individuals, businesses, and industries reach new levels of performance—shows that Microsoft is not just leading the AI revolution, but also shaping the future of how we interact with technology.

For readers, the opportunity to take advantage of these new AI tools is at their fingertips. Whether you are a business leader looking to optimize operations, a student seeking personalized learning experiences, or a professional looking to boost productivity, Microsoft's AI-driven solutions like Copilot offer the power and flexibility to transform how you work and live. The tools are designed to be accessible, adaptable, and user-friendly, making it easy for anyone to integrate them into their daily routines. Now is the time to explore how AI can enhance your productivity, creativity, and decision-making processes.

In this era of rapid technological advancement, Microsoft has ensured that AI is not just a tool for the future—it is a tool for today. By harnessing the power of Copilot and Microsoft's suite of AI-driven solutions, you can unlock new levels of efficiency and innovation in your personal and professional life.

www.ingramcontent.com/pod-product-compliance
Lightning Source LLC
Chambersburg PA
CBHW050308230526
45471CB00005B/2084